COLORING
FLOWERS

OVER 40 DELIGHTFUL PICTURES WITH FULL COLORING GUIDES

ARCTURUS

ARCTURUS

This edition published in 2015 by Arcturus Publishing Limited
26/27 Bickels Yard, 151–153 Bermondsey Street,
London SE1 3HA

ISBN: 978-1-78599-246-9
CH004980US

Printed in China

Introduction

Most of us will have enjoyed coloring in when we were children. Given simple line drawings with big shapes, we grabbed our crayons and set to with enthusiasm. As we became older, though, we were given more grown-up things to do – and when it came to art, there was the anxiety of a blank piece of paper on which to make our own marks, and feel embarrassed because we had got them 'wrong'.

Today, the joy of coloring in has been rediscovered, this time for adults. If you've never tested your artistic talent before, they provide an easy way in, offering the satisfaction of getting a pleasing result – you may decide that your coloring could do with a little refinement next time, but you won't have to worry that your shapes and proportions are so far off course that your subject is hard to recognize.

If flowers are your particular interest, there's no better way to learn than by copying the work of a master. The plates in this book are drawn from *Choix des Plus Belles Fleurs* (Choice of the Most Beautiful Flowers) by Pierre-Joseph Redouté, published in 1827. At one time court artist to Queen Marie Antoinette, Redouté studied botany in depth and illustrated more than 1800 plant species. Today, he remains one of the most famous artists in the genre of botanical painting.

You will probably find that colored pencils are the easiest tools to use here, blending them to achieve a richly colored finish and following the natural direction of the subject's textures, working along the lines of the leaves and petals. Alternatively, try watercolor paints. Buy a small boxed set of the best quality that you can afford, and a watercolor brush with a fine point – a No. 6 round brush is a good general size. With these few simple tools, you'll be equipped to have a go at the blooms that Redouté brought to life two centuries ago.

Diana Vowles

Key: *List of plates*

1 Crown imperial, yellow variety *(Fritillaria imperialis)*

2 Gloxinia variety

3 Amaryllis variety

4 Bunch-flowered narcissus *(Narcissus tazetta)*

5 Japanese camelia *(Camelia japonica)*

6 Tulip *(Tulipa culta)*

7 Common hyacinth *(Hyacinthus orientalis)*

8 Poppy *(Papaver somniferum)*

9 Dutch iris *(Iris × hollandica)*

10 Blanket flower *(Gaillardia)*

11 Snapdragon *(Antirrhinum majus)*

12 Blue false indigo *(Baptisia australis)*

13 Chinese peony
(Paeonia lactiflora)

14 Winged-stem passion
flower *(Passiflora alata)*

15 Knysna lily
(Cyrtanthus obliquus)

16 Fringed iris *(Iris
japonica)*

17 Harlequin flower
(Sparaxis tricolor)

18 Angel's trumpet *(Datura)*

19 Crown imperial
(Fritillaria imperialis)

20 Blue Egyptian water lily
or blue lotus *(Nymphaea
caerulea)*

21 Hanging bells
*(Enkianthus
quinqueflorus)*

22 *Hippeastrum variety*

23 Lady's-slipper orchid
(Cypripedium calceolus)

24 Auricula or mountain
cowslip *(Primula
auricula)*

25 Tulip tree
or Yellow poplar
(Liriodendron tulipifera)

26 Blue plantain lily
*(Hosta ventricosa, formerly
Hemerocallis caerulea)*

27 Sulphur rose
(Rosa hemisphaerica)

28 Sweet pea
(Lathyrus odoratus)

29 Dwarf morning glory
(Convolvulus tricolor)

30 Oleander
(Nerium oleander)

31 Snake vine
(Hibbertia scandens)

32 Heartsease
(Viola tricolor)

33 Cabbage rose
*(Rosa × centifolia
'Bullata')*

34 Common peony
(Paeonia officinalis)

35 Spanish iris
(Iris xiphium variety)

36 Lychnis Coronata
(syn. L. grandiflora)

37 Poppy anemone
or Spanish marigold
(Anemone coronaria)

38 Dahlia *(Dahlia
coccinaea)*

39 Dalmation iris *(Iris
pallida)*

40 Morning glory
(Ipomoea purpurea)

41 Fern-leaf peony
(Paeonia tenuifolia)

42 Nettle-leaved bellflower
(Campanula trachelium)

43 China aster
(Callistephus chinensis)

44 Bouquet of camellias,
narcissus and pansies

1

Fritillaria imperialis

Crown imperial, yellow variety

Gloxinia variety

Gloxinia variety

3

Amaryllis variety

Amaryllis variety

Narcissus tazetta

Bunch-flowered narcissus

Camelia japonica

Japanese camelia

Tulipa culta

Tulip

Hyacinthus orientalis

Common hyacinth

Papaver somniferum

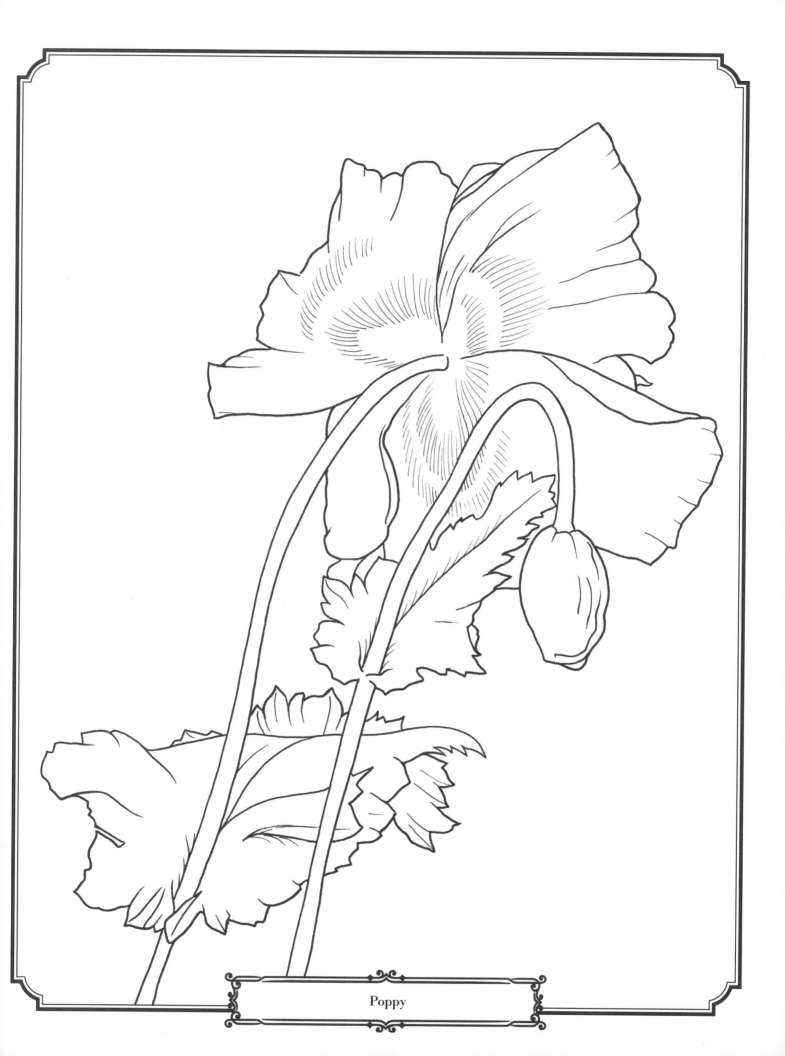

Poppy

Iris × hollandica

Dutch iris

Gaillardia

Blanket flower

Antirrhinum majus

Snapdragon

Baptisia australis

Blue false indigo

Paeonia lactiflora

Chinese peony

Passiflora alata

Winged-stem passion flower

Cyrtanthus obliquus

Knysna lily

16

Iris japonica

Fringed iris

Sparaxis tricolor

Harlequin flower

Datura

Angel's trumpet

Fritillaria imperialis

Crown imperial

Nymphaea caerulea

Blue Egyptian water lily or blue lotus

Enkianthus quinqueflorus

Hanging bells

Hippeastrum variety

Hippeastrum variety

23

Cypripedium calceolus

Lady's-slipper orchid

Primula auricula

Auricula or mountain cowslip

Liriodendron tulipifera

Tulip tree or Yellow poplar

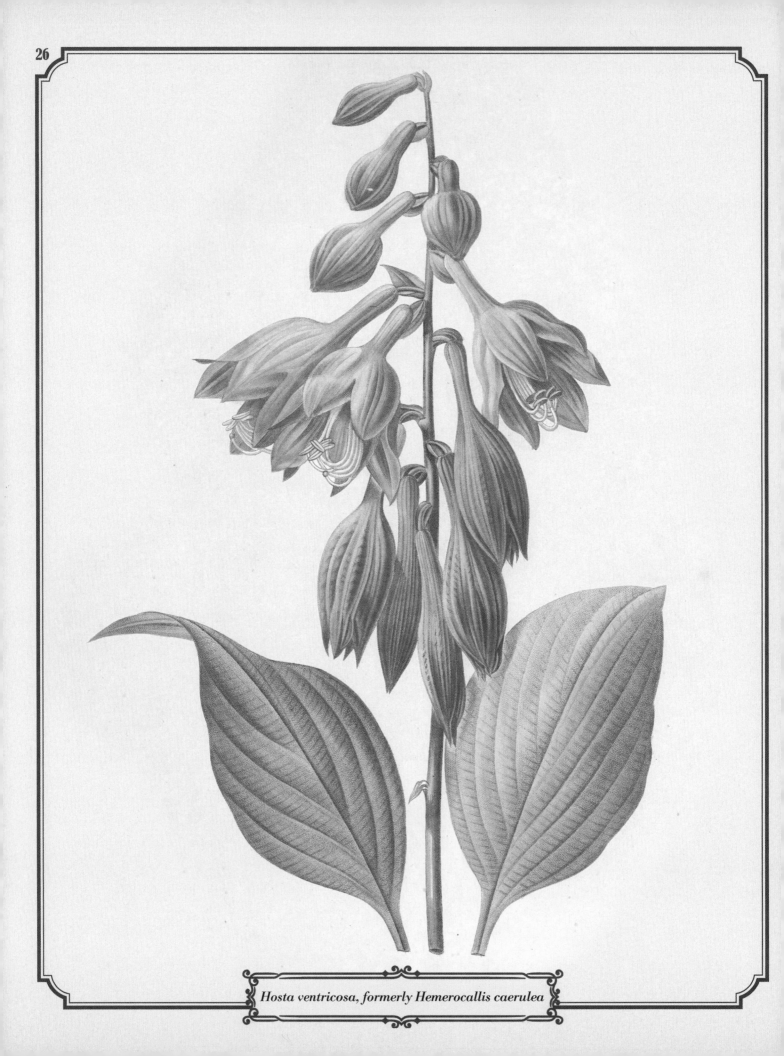

Hosta ventricosa, formerly Hemerocallis caerulea

Blue plantain lily

Rosa hemisphaerica

Sulphur rose

Lathyrus odoratus

Sweet pea

Convolvulus tricolor

Dwarf morning glory

Nerium oleander

Oleander

Hibbertia scandens

Snake vine

Viola tricolor

Heartsease

Rosa × *centifolia* 'Bullata'

Cabbage rose

Paeonia officinalis

Common peony

Iris xiphium variety

Spanish iris

Lychnis Coronata

syn. L. grandiflora

Anemone coronaria

Poppy anemone or Spanish marigold

Dahlia coccinaea

Dahlia

Iris pallida

Dalmation iris

Ipomoea purpurea

Morning glory

Paeonia tenuifolia

Fern-leaf peony

Campanula trachelium

Nettle-leaved bellflower

Callistephus chinensis

China aster

44

Bouquet of camellias, narcissus and pansies

Bouquet of camellias, narcissus and pansies